THE
Big Book
OF
BOWLING

THE Big Book OF BOWLING

HOWARD STALLINGS

With Photographs by
HOWARD STALLINGS
and
MICHAEL NEESE

GIBBS·SMITH
PUBLISHER

SALT LAKE CITY

First edition
97 96 95   8 7 6 5 4 3 2 1
Text copyright ©1995 by Howard Stallings
Photographs ©1995 by Studio Seven Productions/
Howard Stallings

This is a Peregrine Smith Book, published by
Gibbs Smith, Publisher
P.O. Box 667
Layton, Utah 84041

Design by Steven R. Jerman
Jerman Design Incorporated, Salt Lake City
Cover photograph by Michael Neese
Printed and bound in Hong Kong

Library of Congress Cataloging-in-Publication Data
Stallings, Howard.
The big book of bowling / Howard Stallings ;
photographed by Howard Stallings and
Michael Neese.
p.   cm.
ISBN 0-87905-662-2
1. Bowling—United States—History.
2. Bowling—Collectibles—United States—Pictorial
works. I. Neese, Michael. II. Title.
GV902.7.S72   1995
794.6—dc20
94-41020 CIP

Contents

For more than 5,000 years the world has had bowling. Today the sport has touched almost every culture and continent other than Antarctica. Tenpins, the game most Americans think of as bowling, has more than 110 million regular players on six continents, and it is only one of almost a thousand variations played worldwide.

Part of bowling's incredible success lies in the fact that almost anyone can play. The oldest sanctioned bowler in America is 104, and the youngest person to roll a perfect game was only 10 years old. Bowling can also be played almost anywhere. Tenpins is always played on a sixty-foot lane, but there are games that are played on streets and on dirt, and curling is even played on ice.

Before the mid-1950s, tenpin alleys hired pinboys to set up the pins and return the balls to the bowlers. Alleys tended to be dark, smoky places with seedy characters at every turn. With the invention of the automatic pin setters and greater involvement of women, bowling was brought into the sunlight. New centers that sprang up in the suburbs encouraged family fun in a clean and safe environment.

Today, the image of bowling is of a modern, international sport that is played on six continents and is adding almost 1 million new participants every year. It is a sport that looks forward into the future but is rooted firmly in its rich heritage.

The National Bowling Hall of Fame and Museum houses a collection of memorabilia that tells the story of bowling through the ages. It is a fun place to visit and can provide hours of fascinating discovery. We are pleased to cooperate in the creation of this book by lending visual and anecdotal material from our displays and archives. When you're in St. Louis, come by for a visit.

In the meantime, grab your ball and "let's go bowling!"

John Dalzell
Curator of Collections
Bowling Hall of Fame and Museum

The United States is a nation of bowlers. About 79 million of us bowled in 1993 at more than 7,000 bowling centers with more than 160,000 individual lanes. Many of these establishments operate 24 hours a day and offer myriad services, from restaurants and bars to child care and automotive repair. The 231,000 amateur leagues in 1993 alone account for about a billion yearly man/woman-hours on the boards.

Bowling is truly America's most popular participatory sport. It is also a great cultural leveler, attracting people from all age groups, races, religions, and economic strata. "Going bowling" is a joyous social event for most of us, providing an opportunity for safe, pleasant companionship and exercise with friends and family.

It is difficult to describe to a non-bowler the exquisite camaraderie and sheer joy to be found in the bowling alley. It's the wide-open airiness of the space, for one thing, that puts us at ease—no claustrophobia here! Many bowling centers, with their acres of colorful carpet, nicely appointed lounges and restaurants resemble, more than anything else, large, cheerful hotel lobbies. The mood is usually one of festivity, of revelry and gaiety. You know immediately that this is a place designed to deliver good, clean fun. The sounds, too, are somehow very reassuring—the constant, rolling rumble of balls on hardwood boards, the crash and clatter of flying pins, the laughter and chatter.

An air of lightheartedness prevails in all aspects of bowling. Many of us casual bowlers, unlike the serious league players, approach the sport with a sense of mock-seriousness, *almost* never getting uptight about such trivial matters as scores and technique. Oh, sure, we want to better our averages, but never at the expense of the excellent fun.

Whether you are an ardent bowler, a weekend wannabe, or simply an interested observer of the American scene, you will find much to admire in this book: the simple beauty, the dignity and folk-art character of the objects depicted; the rarely told tale of an ancient sport; the superb sense of humor inherent in the bowler's world.

The photographs and objects not only invoke a sense of nostalgia, but they are also important examples of exuberant and colorful Americana.

We hope this book encourages you to evaluate, perhaps for the first time, the familiar *objects d'bowling* around you in a different context. It is meant to be a fun, visual romp through the best collection of bowling memorabilia ever assembled and a shameless extolling of the sport.

7

A Long Time Ago...

WE HUMANS CERTAINLY LOVE to build and create. The act of organizing, classifying, systematizing, of making order from chaos is much of what being human is all about. Conversely, we also like to knock things down, to raze to the ground what once stood as a monument to our logic. This basic urge to build, and then to topple, has evolved over the aeons and is probably more manifest in our nature today than ever before. After all, we have been known to build

These ancient pins and balls, on display at the Bowling Hall of Fame and Museum, were collected throughout Europe during the course of a lifetime.

The earliest supposed bowling implements — balls, pins, and a wicket — found at a child's grave site near Cairo at the turn of this century. These replicas are in the collection of the Bowling Hall of Fame and Museum in St. Louis.

beautiful and elaborate structures — entire cities even —only to turn and smash them down again.

This book, however, is not about anything quite so drastic as leveling cities. It is concerned with this destructive passion only as it relates to the wonderful, age-old sport of bowling, of setting up pins and striking them down again with a ball.

The oldest bowling implements yet unearthed were found by University of London Egyptologist Sir Flinders Petrie about 1900, at an archaeological site near Cairo, dated around 3200 B.C. In his 1939 book, *The Making of Egypt,* Professor Petrie reports that he found the group of objects at a child's grave site—three stone balls, nine conical "pins," and three oblong pieces of marble—and he pronounced them to be toys designed for bowling.

Petrie theorized that the three pieces of marble had formed a type of archway or wicket through which the balls were rolled at the pins, probably arranged in a diamond formation.

The oldest, still-active bowling alley in the U.S. is the Elks Bowling Lanes, Fond du Lac, Wisconsin, first certified in 1909.

According to author Carol Schunk, there is evidence that ancient Romans, about three thousand years later, developed a type of bowling sport derived from a war maneuver. It seems that the Roman army would goad their enemies into a tight mountain pass and bowl them over with large stones rolled down the mountainside. Supposedly, a game of amusement eventually evolved amongst the soldiery, to relive their military exploits and to practice the tactic. This Roman game was one possible source from which many European variations of the sport evolved over the centuries, many of which are still played today.

The Italians, for instance, have their game of *boccie,* in which the player skips, and jumps, much like a discus thrower, then tosses a ball of wood at a steel "washer."

There is one French game, *petanque,* played with a metal ball, and another, *quilles,* played with wooden balls and pins. A Dutch version involves hurling a ball at pins, which are in turn reset by a system of ropes.

In Ireland they play *street bowl,* which involves throwing a steel ball between two points at distances up to five miles apart. The object is to reach the distant point in as few throws as possible.

Some Polynesians developed a game of bowling with rules much like the European model of *bowls.* They played the game in centuries past with a flat stone disc on a court sixty feet long—the same length as modern lanes.

It appears that these children of nobility are playing a form of skittles.
Titled Gallery Over the Hall, Knowle, Kent, *this hand tint is signed, "J. Nash, 1840."*

In another variation in Belgium, a feather, of all things, becomes the mark at which a round ball is rolled. The object of the game, I gather, is to get the closest to the target without crushing it.

The British have for centuries been quite fascinated with a variety of bowling games. In their popular game called *skittles,* which is still played in pubs today, a wooden ball is rolled at a grouping of nine large pins. In some versions of the game, the ball becomes a flattened object shaped like a wheel of cheese. In another version, the player moves in close to drop, or "tip," the ball into the cluster of pins, then moves some distance away to roll into the remainder of pins on a second or spare try.

A nineteenth-century game of kayles, with its kingpin in the center, is pictured in beautiful detail on this British tapestry.

The British game most associated with modern ball-and-pins bowling is the ancient game of *kayles,* very similar to the aforementioned French *quilles,* which means pins. In the French game, the bowler stood close in to the pins and swung the ball for his first try. Then, from a distance, he bowled a spinning ball into the remainder, trying to topple as many as possible. In most versions of *quilles* and *kayles,* the center pin—called the kingpin—was larger and worth more points when upset.

Bowls, or lawn bowling as it is sometimes called, is a time-honored and very blue-blooded English game. Played on lush bowling greens not unlike today's golf greens, this sport incorporates a circular, not spherical, ball with flat sides, which is rolled at an object called a jack, not pins.

King Edward III, in 1366, forbade the game of *bowls* among his troops as they constantly shirked their archery practice in favor of rolling a few balls. Even greater disgrace was attached to the game in London, when in 1455 the world's first-known indoor pin lanes was built and was said to have been frequented by "the dissolute and gamesters." Thus began a long history of repression, especially of the ninepins version, by the aristocracy.

Henry VIII, by some accounts, was a lover of the game, even though he found it necessary, for the good of his wayward subjects, to restrain its practice by statute in 1511. He is said to have built lanes for his own enjoyment at Whitehall Palace. I don't know if Henry's wives approved of his bowling—probably not.

In another attempt to quell the licentious activities associated with bowling, the British monarch enacted another prohibition against it in 1541, which was not repealed until 1845! It said, in part, that all ". . . artificers, labourers, apprentices, servants and the like are forbidden to play bowls except on Christmas and then only in their master's house and presence."

Apparently, however, all attempts to quash the game and the attendant gambling and such failed. The sport's bad reputation continued to build with bowling alley scandals rampant in Elizabethan London. However, the royalty apparently continued to enjoy the sport, encouraging the depravity by example.

It is generally accepted, however, that our modern form of bowling at pins derived most directly from the

Our modern game of tenpins is most directly the descendant of German-style ninepins bowling, as illustrated in this nineteenth-century print by R. Brendamour

13

German game of *kegelspiel* (from which the term *kegeling* is still used to describe the sport). According to German historian William Pehle, in his book *Bowling,* the game originated in the third century as a religious rite associated with symbolically destroying one's enemies. Pehle says parishioners would set up their clublike weapons, called *kegels*, at one end of the cloister and roll a ball to strike them down. The *kegel* was meant to represent the *Heide,* or heathen devil, and he who was most adept at toppling the pagans was praised and lauded as a most exemplary Christian.

Over time, *kegeling* lost much of its original religious significance, though the clergy continued to compete amongst themselves, largely as recreation. It became a common event at all manner of social gatherings such as feast days, weddings, and baptisms, and was popular with nobility and peasants alike. The layout of the "court," the design of balls, and the number of pins were arbitrary in early times, to say the least. The earliest outdoor beds, of packed clay or flat slate, gave way by the 1400s to the use of a single plank of wood, usually not wider than a foot or two. The pins, numbering from as few as three to as many as seventeen, were set up on a slightly wider podium. Such alleys were still in use in Germany into the 1900s.

Just exactly how is not known, but for whatever reason, nine pins set in a diamond formation became the norm as the game expanded into all corners of Germany, as well as into the neighboring countries of Switzerland and Holland.

Through the decades, the various games of bowling at pins gained favor with the common folk, the peasants, in most countries, whereas the games of lawn bowling and the like attracted the more genteel practitioners. The ninepins game came to be associated with the lower classes, bless their hearts, and with drunkenness, gambling, illegal activities, and worse. All over Europe for hundreds of years, settin' 'em up and knockin' 'em down again was the pastime of scoundrels and villains, played as a game for wagering in disreputable alleys out back of taverns and at notorious inns.

It was a game played almost entirely by coarse, roguish men, usually for money. Brawls broke out routinely in these dangerous establishments, and murder was not uncommon. Of course, no self-respecting woman would be caught dead in a bowling alley.

Bowling saloons in Europe and America by the late 1800s were often respectable enough to attract feminine bowlers (and apparently their kids!).
This German painting by L. Blume Siebert catches the mixed double revelers in mid-toast.

15

A GAME OF BOWLS ON BOWLING GREEN, MANHATTAN

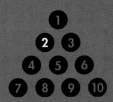

America Goes Bowling

THE EUROPEANS' PASSION FOR bowling continued unabated as they began to establish new colonies in North America. Dutch immigrants, as well as the English and Germans, helped to establish this thoroughly unwholesome amusement very rapidly in the early colonies, irking the church/government here to no end, just as in the Old World. Of course, the straightlaced Puritan colonists sought to forbid all bewitching activities that they thought in some way

Dutch immigrants, the first European inhabitants of Manhattan, brought their love of bowling with them to the New World as shown in this artist's conception from the 1930s.

distracted from the virtuous path—including all forms of ball playing, cards, dancing, backgammon, shuffleboard, and Sunday rides.

Nonetheless, bowling flourished throughout the defiant colonies, with commoners enjoying their ninepins in the alleys out behind the taverns, and the higher classes bowling away on their manicured lawns. The Dutch in mid-seventeenth-century Manhattan established probably the earliest permanent site for bowls, on the southern tip of the island near the battery, or fort, and, as all New Yorkers know, it's still called Bowling Green today. In fact, Bowling Green is a familiar U.S. place-name, as towns tended to evolve around the grassy commons where villagers met to bowl and socialize.

By the turn of the nineteenth century, a steady flow of kegel-loving German immigrants into New York had promptly made that thriving little harbor town into the country's "bowling capital." By the mid-1800s, with continued massive Germanic immigration, bowling with nine pins arranged in a diamond shape was *really* booming, with lawn bowling and the other derivatives left far behind. In a few years, the sport was well established in Midwest cities as well, especially Chicago, and was making inroads all over the country.

Ceramic beer steins decorated with bowling motifs were common German-American awards.

Respectability Comes to the Game

By now, the dual personality of bowling is evident. Originating from religious ritual on one side and from the blood sport of armies on the other, it has, from the outset, been sitting on a moral fence.

This somewhat addictive endeavor, long associated with the vulgar and profane, conforms just as well with the gracious and the cultivated. A nobleman in powdered wig, a drunken serf in pungent rags, a pampered lady in corset and flounces, Church fathers, the children of kings, and the children of farmers have all been smitten by this game over the centuries.

Soon after the end of the bloody Civil War, came another large influx of hard-working, fun-loving German refugees. They organized social and recreational clubs, called *turnvereine*, many with

The oldest continually operating athletic sporting goods company in the U.S. is Brunswick Corporation, founded by Swiss-American John Brunswick in 1845. He was immediately successful, building billiard tables and fine bar fixtures, and soon bought out two competitors to form the Brunswick-Balke-Collender Company.

Adding their line of bowling equipment in 1884 was a natural for the company, a move that helped immeasurably in standardizing the game. The company grew, ultimately producing products as diverse as phonograph records and bathroom fixtures.

It was in 1914 that Brunswick introduced the Mineralite Ball, the fabulous, hard-rubber, high-tech wonder, which, in time, would outsell its competition, but at first required a little fancy promotional footwork to . . . start the ball rolling.

So, Brunswick cooked up a World Tour for their creation, in cooperation with Wells Fargo and YMCA. After surviving numerous mishaps along the way, including its being confiscated by the German military and being presumed lost at sea when its carrier ship went aground near Bombay, the world-hopping wonder-ball finally made it back to the good old USA, after eighteen years and 30,000+ miles.

It was last seen on exhibit at Chicago's "A Century of Progress" in 1934. John Dalzell, curator of the Bowling Hall of Fame and Museum in St. Louis, says that, as of this writing, it's lost again. Its crate, as seen in the photo, is now in the collection of the museum — sans ball!

Brunswick's amazing mineralite ball goes on tour.

bowling lanes. These clubs, generally clean and family-oriented, were the impetus that eventually brought organization and a measure of respect to bowling as a sport.

The scene got a huge, positive boost when the first indoor alley—the *tres chic* Knickerbocker's, with lanes of baked clay—opened in New York City with much fanfare on January 1, 1840. Indoor bowling was an instant craze, and within a decade, as reported by one writer, "On Broadway from Barclay Street to Eighth Street, there were alleys to be found on every block."

Despite the tender underbelly of bowling saloon life, many of the better-run establishments of the last half of the century attracted a higher-class clientele. Even New York society dames, from families such as the Astors, Roosevelts, Stuyvesants, and Vanderbilts, frequented Knickerbocker's. To drop a few more names, Abraham Lincoln, Ulysses S. Grant, R. J. Reynolds, and Mark Twain were all nineteenth-century keglers of note.

Still, in back alleys of urban saloons, continued hustling and gaming during this period prompted increased pressure from the Temperance Society and more government

An evening of tenpins in a reputable alley was a fashionable night out for the gentry of the Gay Nineties, pictured here in Harper's *on January 29, 1892.*

bans in New England against ninepins. But the tide could not be turned. As one theory goes, enterprising proprietors just added another pin to confound the authorities and in no time, ten pins, arranged in the now familiar triangle, became the standard.

Most alleys were dark and cavernous, often found in the chilly, squalid basements of saloons. Inevitably, there would also be pool tables, card tables, bookies, plenty of alcohol, and ladies of the evening to mingle with the male revelers. The fact is, bowling and billiards were there mainly to attract the drinkers, with saloon keepers often giving free games with drink purchases.

The Cleveland armory, where the 1904 ABC was held in the dead of winter, was so badly heated and the roof was so leaky that ice formed on the lanes from melting snow, and the shivering competitors had to bowl in heavy winter gear.

21

Often occupying the basements of saloons, many bowling alleys of the 1870s and '80s were cavernous, ill-lit haunts of a mostly male gambling patronage, ca. 1885.

Attempts to Standardize

During the eighties and nineties, several serious attempts were made by various groups and clubs in New York to standardize the rules and regulations and to clean up their act. Bowling associations in many cities, as a matter of self-defense, tried for decades to attract more women to the sport, a move that eventually did more to legitimize their game than anything else.

In *The Perfect Game*, Herman Weiskopf quotes a story in a Milwaukee paper about one such attempt:

> The ladies who passed through Burns' swinging doors took a shocked look at the joint and told the proprietor it would never do if he wanted the feminine trade. Spittoons went out, the genuine oil paintings of naked nymphs came down from behind the bar, curtains were hung, and rugs laid. The help were ordered to shave at least twice a week. Signs went up asking patrons to kindly refrain from profane language.

This turn-of-the-century advertising illustration is from a Chicago bowling journal. It reflects a respectable image for the game.

As attested to by this 1899 New York Herald feature, bowling clubs by this time had become fashionable, high-society hangouts.

Early twentieth-century lady bowlers take over the alley for a tournament.

Bowling, of course, was not the only sport struggling for legitimacy in Victorian America. The sports regularly covered in the *New York Times* during the 1890s were billiards, biking, bowling, and that other great American pastime—baseball. It was not unusual for men to be members of teams from more than one discipline at the same time, especially bowling and baseball.

Three generations of Lubys are in the ABC Hall of Fame: David Luby, Mort Luby, Jr., and Mort Luby, Sr.

As a matter of fact, some of the founding fathers of bowling were pioneers as well in civilizing the sport of baseball. For instance, A. G. Spalding, author of the 1887 *Standard Rules for Bowling in the United States,* was instrumental in the formation of baseball's National League.

American Bowling Congress Formed

Into the turmoil walked a young German immigrant, Joe Thum, the "Father of Bowling." In 1869, Thum arrived in New York at age fifteen and went to work at a Bavarian restaurant, which later became his when the homesick owner returned to his native Germany.

In 1886, Joe opened his first successful alley in the basement of the restaurant; then in 1891, he built six more lanes at Germania Hall. In 1901, he opened the world's most elegant alley, with expensive state-of-the-art lanes, innovative electric lighting, and extravagant interior design, and called it the White Elephant, after his detractors prematurely pronounced it a disaster.

Thum, disgusted with the chaos surrounding his beloved sport, managed, with considerable cajoling, to convince the ornery New York proprietors and other leaders to organize and to accept a uniform set of rules and specifications distilled from past attempts.

With the terrific woodworking and the latest in equipment and newfangled electric lighting, this Newport, Kentucky, alley must have been quite a showplace ca. 1904.

The resulting United Bowling Clubs (UBC), by the mid-1890s, had around 120 members—real progress was finally underway. Thum, with the help of New York's *Bowler's Journal*, pushed for a national organization. Bowling leaders in the twenty or so other bowling cities took note. Not-so-friendly debates, on a variety of sectional rivalries between the West and East, broke out in a number of start-up bowling journals but were overcome long enough to allow for face-to-face negotiations.

In four separate organizational sessions in 1895 and

Dave Luby's Bowler's Journal, *first published in November 1913 and surviving heartily today, served during various periods as the official publication of both the ABC and the Bowling Proprietors Association of America (B.P.A.A.).*

T H E   F I R S T   A B C   T O U R N E Y

You might say that the first ABC Tournament in January 1901 was a test of giant Teutonic wills. Amid continued bickering between the eastern and western factions, a suitable location was selected, a 50' x 165' six-lane alley on Chicago's Wabash Avenue, close by the Masonic Lodge location of the ABC Convention.

With seating for only 800, this first National Bowling Championship was an easy sellout. The four-day competition attracted 41 teams, 78 doubles, and 115 singles entries from nine states. The overflow crowd was very noisy—though civil—and was appreciative of the drama of the sharp competition.

The homeboy Standard Club took the team prize of $200, and Frank Brill, Chicago's tournament organizer, won the Singles and All-events titles. The Big Apple's John Voorhies and C. K. Starr took the Doubles $80 pot.

The competition was contentious, spiteful, perhaps even malicious at times, and it would take a few more years yet for those old boys and their bowling Congress to totally grow up. But it was an auspicious and fruitful beginning there in Chicago during those first few cold days of the twentieth century.

January 1896, the rancorous national leaders met at Beethoven Hall in New York City to form the sport's national governing body, the American Bowling Congress (ABC), and to set rules, regulations, and equipment specs. The ABC today recognizes the date of September 9, 1895, as its official inauguration.

In 1945, Louis Stein, last surviving attendee of the first ABC meetings, described them like this in a *Bowling Magazine* article:

> Bowlers interested in the advancement of their favorite sport met on several occasions seeking to standardize the game. We exchanged theories, but didn't seem to be getting anywhere. . . .
>
> We decided to do something definite. So this meeting at Beethoven Hall was called and we agreed to stay in session until we had accomplished our aims. That was a long session, consuming 15 hours as I recall. We ate dozens of sandwiches and finished six ponies of beer. When [rules committeeman] W. W. Ward hit upon the name, American Bowling Congress, it was the signal to tap another barrel.

A rare photo from 1897 pictures New York's Lexington Bowling Club with a couple of pinboys.

Well, nothing much happened until 1899, when most of the national ABC delegates assembled in Union City, New Jersey, to participate in a UBC-sponsored tournament. It was there that the seeds for a truly national ABC tourney were planted.

At the 1900 ABC meeting in Baltimore, Chicagoan Godfred Langhenry convinced the delegates to come to his windy city for not only the next session, but also for a major national tournament. So it happened that the first "super bowl," the initial ABC bowling free-for-all, pitting the haughty New Yorkers against the upstart Midwesters, took place in Chicago in January 1901, the first month of the new century, nearly three years before the inaugural World Series of baseball.

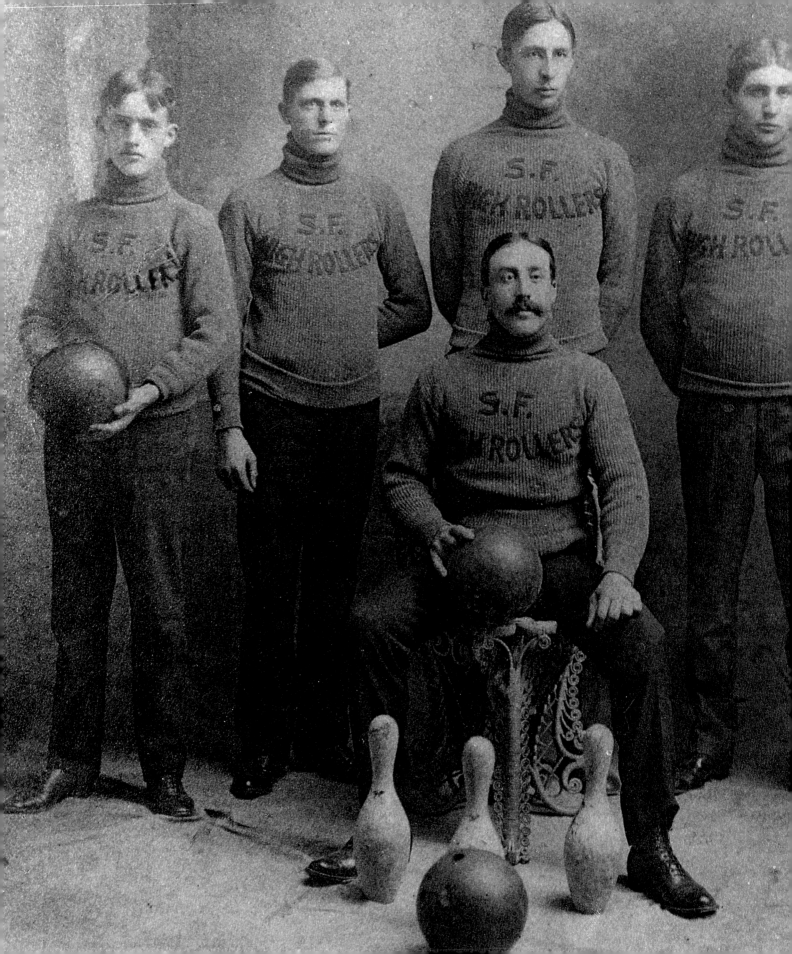

29

A late-nineteenth-century beech ball with two maple pins. There is something very pleasing, sculpturally, about these objects together.

Capitol Bowling Club

ST. PAUL MINNESOTA

This handsome St. Paul, Minnesota, club pin from ca. 1900 is of celluloid and bronze.

30

Nineteenth-century bowlers received some of the most beautiful and expensive
trophies ever produced. This ball-and-pin trophy from 1897 is silver plate, and the cup
from 1886 is a sterling design by Tiffany, executed by Rogers Silver.

This beautifully weathered octagonal wooden box, dated ca. 1905,
is the earliest example of carrying paraphernalia in the collection of the Bowling Hall
of Fame and Museum. Maker of the piece is unknown.

Grüss von der WM '86 in München

GUT HOLZ!

Season's Greetings

13. Bowling Girl

COPYRIGHT, 1903, J. DE YONCH

You will succeed according to
your wishes,
My Valentine.

Bowling Comes of Age

IN ITS FIRST FEW YEARS of existence, the American Bowling Congress (ABC) was mired in continued feuding between the eastern and western factions. There was haggling over rules, voting procedures, lane and equipment regulations, dues, and salaries; but the most irksome disagreement of all was over the use of the infamous "dodo ball." The dodo, extensively used by western bowlers, was heavier and biased—that is, loaded with extra weight on

Try to imagine a time when one of these very special greeting cards might turn up in your mailbox, with tales of a happy time at an ABC tourney. These highly collectible specimens are dated from 1886 to about 1905.

the hitting side. The erratic action of the loaded ball has been described as something like the wobbling of a dying top; but it was effective, delivering more power to the pins at impact. Eastern bowlers, to say the least, were a bit infuriated when its use came to light.

Together, the men's ABC and women's WIBC associations have about five million members.

An editorial in New York's UBC *Bowler's Journal* in February 1903 angrily declared, "The loaded ball is certainly something new, at least for New Yorkers, who had no idea what kind of bunco game they were up against at Buffalo and Toledo." A cry was heard throughout the land: "The dodo ball must go!"

When regulations were adopted outlawing the dodo in 1904 – 05, the desire for harmony finally prevailed and the nation's bowlers set about in earnest to unify the sport and to present a more wholesome image. The ambience of bowling alleys was made somewhat more pleasurable with electric lighting and hand-loaded, semiautomatic pinsetters.

Credit must be given to the ABC and the dedicated individual organizers who worked to clean up the sport. The annual staging of the elaborate National Tournament underscored their seriousness.

Women's bowling evolved right alongside, sometimes a few steps ahead of, the men's. St. Louis proprietor Dennis J. Sweeney instituted the first women's leagues in 1907, and staged the first women's informal national tournament that year as well, the day before the ABC on

By 1916, this state-of-the-art San Francisco alley had installed the semiautomatic pinsetters, which, unfortunately, were still loaded by pinboys.

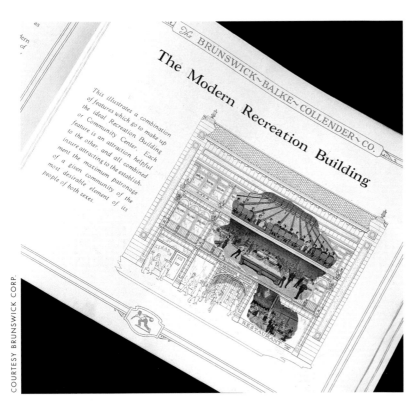

In a cutaway catalog illustration from the 1920s, Brunswick demonstrates the tri-story construction of the "Ideal Recreation Building."

the same lanes. After two more exhibition championships in 1911 and 1916, the newly formed Women's International Bowling Congress (WIBC) held its first official tournament at the ABC lanes in Cincinnati in 1918. The WIBC provided the same type of organization, legitimacy, and impetus for growth to America's feminine bowlers as did the ABC for men.

Prosperity and Depression

As the twenties roared in, so did America's first great "youth rebellion." F. Scott Fitzgerald wrote, "The uncertainties of 1919 were over. America was going on the greatest, gaudiest spree in history."

The fruits of the Industrial Age fueled an economic boom in this country just after World War I. High-quality consumer goods were affordable and plentiful. Corporate profits were way up. A giddy, euphoric public, convinced of an ever-expanding prosperity, piled up credit and invested heavily in get-rich-quick speculation.

A new sophistication was manifest in the first generation of Americans to come of age in the twentieth century. The kids liked their automobiles, cigarettes and booze, their daring clothes and wacky hairdos, sexy dances and late-night parties—and the "degenerate sounds" of jazz. Walter Fabian wrote in *Flaming Youth*, "They're all desperadoes, these kids, all of them with any life in their veins; the girls as well as the boys; maybe

Hall of Famer Johnny Crimmins donned a black, hooded mask and bowled pro-wrestler style as the Masked Marvel from the 1920s through the 1940s.

35

more than the boys." Sound familiar?

Perhaps it was a backlash effect to this new permissiveness that, in part, brought about the Prohibition Act, making alcoholic drinks illegal throughout the country.

Though the pro-hibition was flagrantly violated and American alcohol consumption act-ually increased in the twenties, you could no longer get a drink in the nation's bowling alleys. Faced with major losses in alcohol sales, propri-etors were forced to experiment with more creative ideas to attract the family business. Slowly but surely, mass America was lured by the pure pleasures of this affordable, accessible sport, and the dry alleys were, at last, fit for the wife and kids.

In the Roaring Twenties, multistory urban entertainment complexes, anchored by a bowling/billiard establishment such as Dwyer's in this photo, were dominant. Note the Bohemia and Arcadia dance halls and restaurants on the first floor.

Of course, most alleys at that time were still urban affairs. Three-story design was common, with restaurants and sometimes night clubs or dance halls on the street floor, billiards on the second, and bowling on the top.

In 1920 there were about 450 ABC-sanctioned alleys in the U.S. That figure jumped to about 2,000 by the end of the decade. Then, in 1929, as we all know, the bubble burst, the bloated stock market crashed, and the era which has come to be known as the Great Depression began.

Faced with the harsh economic realities of the thirties, with falling league memberships and low revenues, the nation's operators banded together to form the Bowling Proprietor's Association of America (BPAA) to explore ways to better promote the game. Their group efforts, with innovative national promotions, incentives, and tournaments during those most difficult times, helped to keep alive the momentum gained in the twenties.

The repeal of Prohibition in 1933 provided a huge boost. Though pleased with the prospects of renewed alcohol sales, the BPAA was eager not to revert back to the "saloon image." Revived U.S. brewers, likewise, sought opportunities to project a more honorable public image. The two industries joined forces, with breweries signing up to

Believe it or not, in 1929 Skang Mercurio bowled 65 consecutive errorless games, missing the tenpin in the ninth frame of game 66.

37

Some of the greatest bowlers of their day, the Chicago-based Duffy Florals for several years held the unofficial team championship, which was determined by challenge play among Classic Leaguers. (Standing, left to right): Hall of Famer Eddie Krems, Dom DeVito, and Hank Marino, also a Hall of Famer; (seated): Bill Brennan and Joe Fliger.

sponsor bowling teams in the hope that the brewery's name would be mentioned in sports columns.

Stroh's Bohemian Brewery of Detroit was the first brewer to sponsor a nationally successful bowling team, winning their first of five B.P.A.A team titles in 1934, the year after the repeal of Prohibition.

To this day, breweries have continued their welcome, heavy sponsorship of the sport, and bowling centers are still popular watering holes. With a strong public will to severely restrain drinking (and smoking) in many secular establishments, the industry continues to wrestle with the age-old sobriety dilemma—how to balance the demand for wholesome, family sport and entertainment with the desire for carefree, social imbibing.

By the mid-thirties bowling was rapidly gaining newer, much cleaner appeal. With its superstars decked out in the spotless white and cream-colored uniforms favored by beer sponsors, they looked like milkmen! Emphasis was increasingly placed on the healthful aspects of the exercise involved. The *Journal of the American Medical Association* reported, ". . . many physicians recommend bowling, for it exercises unused muscles of the body and can be played year-round."

Bowling houses began to modernize, tearing down or redecorating the old Victorian alleys and updating their look. Uncomfortable,

Vogue Recreation
Detroit, Michigan

Streamline Moderne, or Deco design, beautifully realized in the 1930s Vogue Recreation Bowling Center in Detroit, Michigan, was representative of the optimistic, technology-inspired spirit of the times.

hardback chairs were replaced with sleek, upholstered furnishings, and the streamlined look of Art Deco became dominant in the new metal and glass architecture and equipment of that era. In short, bowling lanes took on a glitzy, fashionable aura. The Roxy lanes on Fiftieth Street in Manhattan was described by one reporter as having "a Hollywood-Broadway look, a ninety foot oval bar and a swank lobby bedecked with photographs of movie stars, models and major league baseball stars." Ooh, la-la!

The imagery and implements of bowling—the glossy, hard ball speeding down a super-slick, blonde, wooden surface, smashing into mathematically arranged, streamlined pins—meshed perfectly with the era's "need for speed," the aerodynamic zeitgeist, if you will. It may have been largely subconscious, but bowling was definitely perceived as a futuristic pursuit. Its imagery was the epitome of Art Deco, the school of design characterized by rounded edges, smooth surfaces, and low, horizontal profiles.

D R O P   M E   A   P O S T C A R D ,
S E N D   M E   A   L I N E

Postal cards featuring the bowling motif date back at least to the last decade of the nineteenth century, when teams and individuals began to publish photo cards as handy, mailable advertisements that could double as calling cards. Humorous and often naughty cartoons, word plays, and cornball punning soon became popular themes for these "penny postcards," as did travel subjects with bowling artwork.

Expensively produced Christmas, valentines, and other special-occasion cards from around the world can be found adorned with gorgeous Victorian, Art Nouveau, Art Deco, and Impressionist-styled litho reproductions.

Cards promoting the American Bowling Congress were published, with wide-angle photos of the specially constructed, early grand "palaces," replete with the latest in equipment and decorated with bunting and flags.

Bowling alley owners also got into the act, printing and distributing elaborate, linen-surface cards to publicize their establishments. Collecting these rare bits of bowling ephemera might be the most fun of all, because you're sometimes rewarded with a tiny handwritten slice of life and a dated postmark as a free bonus!

Vintage photo postcards from the wee years of the twentieth century. Martin Kern, decked out in his team shirt, suspenders, and plaid pants was the 1904 American Bowling Congress (ABC) champion. The stiffly posed Emma Jeager was a much-respected founding member and three-time champion of the Women's International Bowling Congress (WIBC).

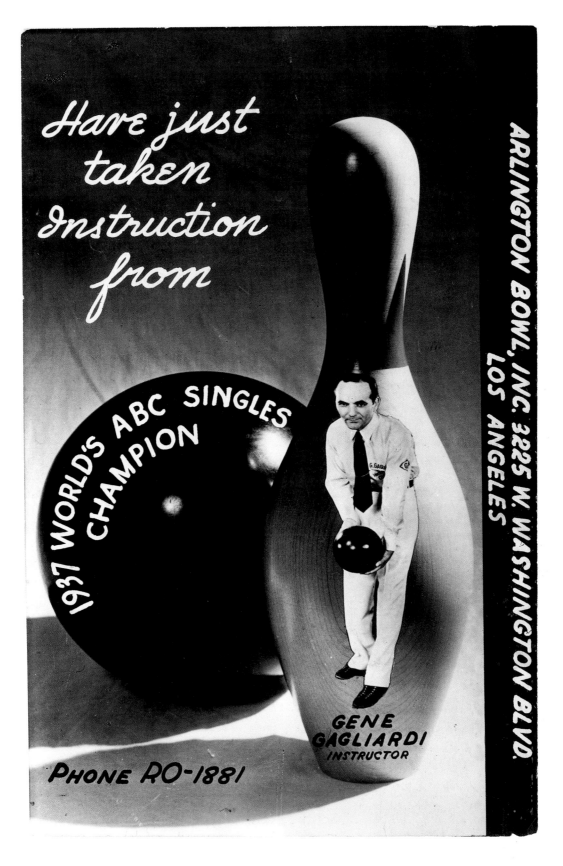

This souvenir postcard from pro champ and instructor Gene Gagliardi
worked handily as a snazzy business card.

A lovely souvenir card of the ABC tournament in Milwaukee, 1923.
Excellent photography by Kaufmann and Fabry, New York.
I must tell you, I'm amazed—everyone's in dark suits! Name a sporting
event that garners such respect today.

Below are two fine examples of cards reproduced from original paintings.
The one on the left is postmarked July 1900, but the other is undated.

Right: I love the corny humor and the lively cartooning illustrated in this
selection of postcards dating from 1906 to 1957. Those little cats kill me!

ANNUAL
CHICAGO
MEN'S
INDIVIDUAL
MATCH GAME
CHAMPIONSHIP

BUDDY BOMAR
1943
CHAMPION

SPONSORED BY
CHICAGO BOWLING COUNCIL
AND THE
BOWLING PROPRIETORS ASSOCIATION
OF
GREATER CHICAGO

The Glory Years

WITH THEIR MEN AWAY

for extended periods of time during the World War II years of the 1940s, women were attracted to the suddenly glamorous sport of bowling in much larger numbers.

Patriotism was very high in the bowling industry, and BPAA took the lead among sports associations in endorsing various fund-raising schemes and selling war bonds. The WIBC was especially active, organizing nationwide fund drives for donations to the armed services.

Opposite: Trophy clocks were a popular trend for a while. Too bad we don't see these extraordinary items on mantles anymore.

Where other sports floundered during the depression and war years, the bowling industry prospered.

Gilbert Bailey in the *New York Times Magazine* reported in April 1949 that there were "uncounted thousands of alleys in lodgehalls, industrial plants, private homes, universities and, of course, church basements, where the game is sometimes played to raise money for the preacher's salary."

The boys overseas were bowling like crazy, too. It was reported that in occupied Germany alone, the American GIs formed 500 leagues.

During W.W.I.I. women bowlers raised funds through their favorite sport to pay for Air Force bombers and other equipment, like Miss W.I.B.C., being christened here in 1943.

The momentum gained during World War II in the bowling industry continued unabated as the returning servicemen searched out avenues for relaxation, camaraderie, and amusement. Along with the famous Baby Boom, the less-famous Bowling Boom was underway.

In 1949, for example, there were no less than 58 bowling centers in Manhattan alone and 6,097 nationwide, compared to about 1,450 in 1920, the year Prohibition was enacted. Also, in 1949, 5,444 teams from 42 states competed at the Atlantic City ABC, whereas in 1920, 20 states yielded only 900 teams. Those bowling alleys were hopping!

The *New York Times Magazine* reported in 1949, "If it's any comfort to people who think

It's 1942 and America pumps up for the war effort with "healthful recreation."

the devil has got the big cities, bowling alleys outnumber dance pavilions three to one in a three square-block area just North of Times Square."

Technology to the Rescue

However, the best was yet to come, triggered largely by the introduction of two very different but equally momentous technological breakthroughs: the long-awaited, fully automatic pinsetter, and the great cultural leveler of the twentieth century, the electronic opiate of the masses—television.

In 1953 Allen Wells of Charleston, West Virginia, bowled a perfect game without seeing the pins. As a special promotion, an opaque curtain was hung across the lane to obscure the bowler's view—and he nailed it!

Granny Gets a Strike, *by Hy Hintermeister, ca. 1945.*

It is difficult to exaggerate the importance of pinsetting automation to the flowering of the industry. Its invention was no doubt the pivotal event in all of bowling history. The main thing that had held bowling back and prevented its full-fledged entry into middle-class respectability was the industry's reliance on scarce, unreliable pin-boys—those slovenly, profane creatures who manned the "pits," reloading the lanes as it were.

The fact that it was menial, repetitive, and thankless labor added to the pinboy's notoriously bad attitude and demeanor. However, to be fair to the pinboys of the world, by this time the occupation had been cleaned up considerably. Pinboys had organized and even unionized, with nearly 5,000 members in the New York area. Many centers employed teenagers, as well—after school and on weekends—but they were still in very short supply.

Once the pinsetting procedure was automated, bowling lanes began to move with precision, and many more games could be bowled in a day's time than were possible before. Profits went up. Customers were happier.

The company that first produced pinsetter automation was American Machine and Foundry (AMF), which previously had made machinery for the apparel, tobacco, and bakery industries. AMF had the foresight to purchase the patent rights from the inventor, Gottfried Schmidt, in 1945. Wartime production needs delayed the project, but by 1952 the first refined, fully operational system was installed at the sixteen-lane Farragut Pool Lanes in Brooklyn.

Suffice it to say that the new bowling product line did wonders for AMF's stockholders! It was several years before

COURTESY BRUNSWICK CORPORATION

Catalog touts glamorous spectator facilities, 1940s.

longtime bowling manufacturer Brunswick got their pinsetter system to market and began to recover from the dramatic setback.

With automation on line, the sport literally exploded like a splasher in the tenth frame, and a great sigh of relief was heard throughout bowling-land. With the new technology, alleys (now generally referred to as Bowling Centers) swung into 24-hour operation. Women's league play dominated the morning and early afternoon hours, followed by the eager kids after school. Then came the early evening leagues for dad and grandpa, and finally, late night and the wee hours for night owls and insomniacs.

In May 1947, at about the same time that Harry Truman

The legendary Budweiser team of 1957 – 58 holds the record for the most 300 games by a team in one season, at seven.

President Harry S. Truman enjoys himself on the lanes that he had installed in the White House in the eventful year of 1947.

installed lanes in the White House, *Life* magazine claimed that bowling was the most popular U.S. participatory sport and that 18,500,000 American bowlers spent $200 million in 1946 for balls, bags, shoes and fees. *Life* also painted a Rockwellian picture of America's bowlers in a 1948 article: "Once a week a timorous shoe clerk can . . . put on a brightly colored shirt, rub chalk on his hands and face up to the pins. And on that unforgettable night when he pulls his team out of a hole with three strikes in the tenth frame, he really becomes an Andy Varipapa."

The magazine, incidentally, listed their choices for the "Ten Best Bowlers" in that article as Andy Varipapa, Joe Wilman, Buddy Bomar, Paul Krumske, Ned Day, Tony Sparando, Junie McMahon, Joe Norris, Walter Ward, and George Young.

By pure, sweet coincidence, 1947 was also the year that commercial television arrived on the American scene, an infant broadcast industry desperately in search of programming to send out to those tiny eight- and ten-inch screens across the

THE ST. LOUIS SHUFFLER

Don Carter is generally considered to be the sport's biggest star and perhaps the greatest bowler who ever lived. He dominated bowling during its heyday in the 1950s.

The "St. Louis Shuffler," so called due to his unorthodox crouching approach to the line and his bent-elbow delivery, racked up the most impressive career statistics in history. To start with, he won four All-Star championships, five World Invitational titles, six PBA championships, and was six times named Bowler of the Year—not to mention his legendary team play. Since an early retirement in 1972, hastened by serious knee problems, he has served three terms as PBA president.

Carter's position as one of TV's first media superstars was created in part by his dominance of '50s and early '60s bowling shows. In 1964, he became the first athlete ever to sign a million-dollar contract—with Ebonite, to promote their equipment.

The likable and soft-spoken Carter jokes that he is "the only guy to have two wives in the WIBC Hall of Fame (ex-wife LaVerne and present wife Paula)." Today he lives near Miami, Florida. Don remains active in the family's bowling center business.

In 1994, at age sixty-eight, with his ailing knees fully reconstructed, Carter returned to organized bowling after a twenty-two-year hiatus. As reported in *Bowling Magazine*, "He isn't interested in headlines. He merely wanted to bowl in a summer league with his foster son, John, 13."

Carter and ABC Secretary Emeritus Frank Baker were special honorees at the Bowling Hall of Fame and Museum's Salute to Champions, which culminated the March 1995 Centennial ABC Convention in Reno, Nevada.

U.S. Lacking the technology to effectively cover high-action sports, the fledgling TV networks soon discovered that televising a bowling event was a cakewalk. Good close-ups were easy, showing intensity, emotion, suspense—and the game was all-season, indoors, and already pretty well lit!

It was in that same year of 1947 that the very first bowling show was telecast from the Capitol Health Center near Times Square in Manhattan to viewers of CBS's Channel 2, within a mighty radius of fifty miles. The program was an instant success. (Of course, there wasn't much competition on the airwaves that year.) Bowling shows popped up overnight as Americans bought their TVs by the millions and tuned in to watch the big stars like Don Carter, Buddy Bomar, and Carmen Salvino walk away with the big prize money.

The relationship of these two industries was truly symbiotic in those halcyon days, each feeding off the other for survival at this critical juncture of history.

It was all these factors working together in mid-century America that produced the enormous bowling boom in the 1950s and early 1960s. That era saw tremendous increases in every aspect of the sport, with American Bowling Congress membership increasing fourfold, from 1,105,000 in 1947 to 4,575,000 in 1963. This dramatic influx of new members, not to mention the 20 to 25 million casual bowlers, spurred a tremendous building surge, with the total number of sanctioned U.S. lanes rising from 44,500 to 159,000 during those same years.

The record for the most gutter balls in one game is held by Richard Caplette of Danielson, Connecticut, for his 19 consecutive beauties.

Ed Lubanski, ABC Hall of Famer, had to withdraw from a Niagara Falls tourney in 1984 when his ball rolled off the motel bed and broke his toe.

Searchlights accent the sky at Grand Opening night of Santa Monica's stylish and trendy Llo-Da-Mar lanes, a spectacular mid-forties, Deco-styled establishment owned by, and named for, actor Harold Lloyd and bowling stars Ned Day and Hank Marino.

Remember, this was before the BIG MALL era. The new million-dollar, luxurious suburban bowling centers gave Middle America somewhere to go—somewhere nice and flashy, with rock 'n' roll on the Rock-ola jukebox, with hamburgers and French fries, with cocktails for Mom and Dad and pinball for the kids. Most successful centers were, literally, 24-hour entertainment meccas—fifties style. They were cool!

There was Ike to like, and Willie Mays, '57 Chevies and Marilyn Monroe. You could watch a 3-D movie, hula-hoop, or stuff a wild bikini. There were sputniks and air-raid shelters, Roy Rogers and Davy Crockett. There were Lucy and Ricky, Matt and Miss Kitty, Dick Clark and Elvis the Pelvis. You could Twist, have a barbecue, watch the Green Bay Packers or—grab your chick and GO BOWLING!

The Buds whoop it up after a world's record scoring win in 1958. The legendary Budweiser St. Louis All-Stars, 1957–58, perhaps the greatest bowling team of all time, were (left to right) Don Carter, Tom Hennessey, Ray Bluth, Dick Weber, and Pat Patterson.

Mike Kappa of Racine, WI, holds the title for the worst score ever in league play. He bowled a 2 in 1981. Mike, how?

Newsweek reported the opening of the Joe Kirkwood Bowling Center like this: "On Los Angeles's Ventura Boulevard, klieg lights speared the sky, an exalted crowd jostled for glimpses of celebrities, and TV cameras zeroed in to thrill home viewers with live closeups."

Mr. TV, Milton Berle, handed out big money on his popular show, *Jackpot Bowling.* Television and film stars of the day matched their skills each week on *Celebrity Bowling.* In addition, there were *Championship Bowling, Make That Spare,* and *Bowling for Dollars.* Ozzie and Harriet liked to bowl. So did Jerry Lewis and Ralph Cramden. Of course, there was ABC's wildly successful *Pro Bowler's Tour,* the second longest-running sports series on TV.

The *New York Times* reported, "Tenpin enthusiasts maintain that last year (1957) television devoted more time—9,000 hours—to bowling than to any other sport. Chicago had seven programs a week, while New York ran four and Detroit three. . . . On TV, bowling is like a quiz show with muscle."

The most fouls ever in one league game —15 — were committed by Bud Mathieson, Ocean Beach, California, on December 30, 1946

Members of the big '50s teams, like the Budweisers and the Falstaffs, became sport superstars, largely due to television. The opening telecast of *Celebrity Bowling*, when Ned Day defeated Buddy Bomar, made headlines across the country. Don Carter went on the show and became a "public idol" when he went unbeaten for eight straight weeks. Marion Ladewig, who dominated '50s women's competition, was a media sensation.

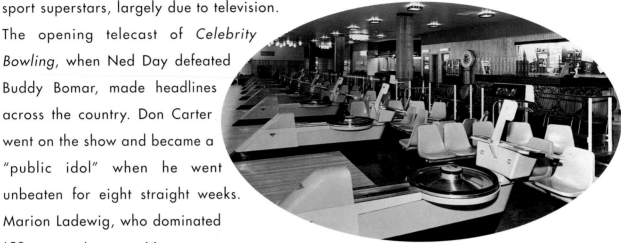

A classic, late-1950s interior view of an AMF supplied center at the peak of the bowling boom years.

Jet Age Bowling Center Design

No doubt about it, TV coverage threw fuel on the bowling bonfire and pulled U.S. couch potatoes into the ritzy new centers by the millions. Larry Mattson, an AMF manager, quipped in a *Newsweek* article, "People who never bowled before saw pretty housewives weighing 98 pounds toppling the maples—and figured, 'I can too'."

In March 1958, America's communal voice, *Life* magazine wrote:

The American Bowling alley, once stuck shamefacedly in a back-street basement, has acquired a stunning elegance and has bloomed into an all-purpose pleasure palace offering a variety in entertainment and luxury.

All the elements of mid-century style came together in this interior from the AMF 1962-63 catalog.

Its facades have the glitter of a Hollywood nightclub. Its deep-carpeted lobbies are lined with restaurants, cocktail lounges, billiard and beauty parlors. . . . As a result the game that was once a man's excuse for a night out has become a place where he takes the whole family.

Buffalo, New York's Suburban Lanes, a spectacular two-million-dollar outfit, attracted the family trade with some novel ideas and promotions. The play and spectator areas were equipped with built-in "wall cribs," and they provided a well-maintained outdoor barbecue patio and swimming pool. The management also rewarded perfect games with free family trips to the Virgin Islands.

Frank Esposito's 42-lane Paramus, New Jersey, center was another family showplace. It had spiffy wall-to-wall carpet, a cozy cocktail bar, a diner with foot-longs to die for, and a nursery with closed-circuit TV, so Mom could bowl and watch

Jane Wyman, later Mrs. Ronald Reagan, lent a little Hollywood glitz to this Deco bowling mag cover.

THE BOWLING REPORTER
· · · PUBLISHED MONTHLY FOR · · ·
THE PLAYDIUM
IN THE INTERESTS OF BOWLERS AND BOWLING

AUGUST, 1940

By the early sixties, bowling had totally completed its metamorphosis from raunchy, tavern amusement to decent and wholesome family entertainment and professional sport. Sparkling clean, safe and inexpensive, the best of the '50s and '60s centers provided the perfect place to take the kids.

Buy where you bowl

BOWLING IS FUN FOR THE WHOLE FAMILY

COURTESY AMF CORPORATION

Junior at the same time. Esposito called his extravaganza, "a country club open to the public."

As a matter of fact, many country clubs and some corporations did build their own lanes. One survey reported that, ". . . 97 percent of the nation's industrial companies foot the bills for their employees bowling."

Many in the industry, buoyed by the sudden, wild popularity of bowling in the fifties, became overconfident. Unmindful of the marked cyclical nature of the sport's history, the changing social climate in the country, and disregarding the inevitable bust that was to follow, the bowling industry began to collapse of its own weight in the early sixties. (Story continues on page 85.)

COURTESY AMF CORPORATION

AMF published this bright and classic fashion catalog for the 1961–62 season, a year which marked the beginning of the end of what has come to be known as "the golden age of bowling."

B O W L I N G   W E A R

Bowling attire, especially the richly embroidered shirts of the 1910s through the 1950s, is undoubtedly the most collectible memorabilia associated with the sport. Collectors and lovers of vintage clothing throughout the country treasure their unique and singular characteristics, the bold and witty graphics, and unusual patterning.

Team shirts or dresses, which were produced in very small quantities, are rare and precious, with the bowlers' names and patches further individualizing each piece. They are priceless keepsakes of times past and highly personal mementos of our parents' or grandparents' happy days with friends at the lanes.

The droll and inventive team logos and other artwork attest to the engaging sense of humor of America's bowlers. Really goofy sponsor ads, intentionally dumb cartooning, girlie spoofs, and just downright silly visual gags were favored. Other shirts depicting straightforward graphics with primitive clip-art designs and block or script lettering are today just as endearing to collectors.

The earliest team shirts from the turn of the century were constructed of standard materials and seem to have been based on the baseball shirt model. The customary cut of a classic bowling shirt included loose tailoring, side and sleeve vents for easy arm movements, and an open collar. Two-tone colorations became quite popular as did the use of ornate buttons and pocket emblems. Bowlers often wore dress clothes and shoes to important competitions; dark suits with white shirts were the norm—very dignified, you see. Later, silk was a popular shirt fabric for men and dress fabric for women. Satin, linen, challis, gabardine, rayon, and other fine man-made materials, as well as cotton, were also prevalent.

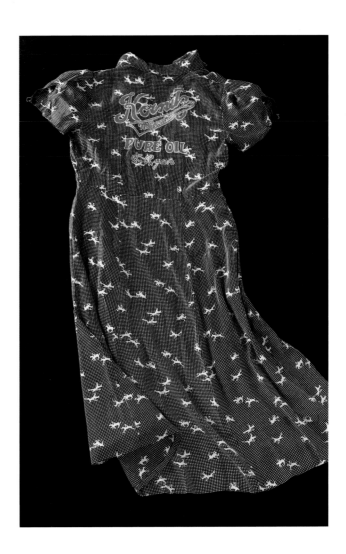

Though quite fashionable, the bowling shirts and dresses chosen by women bowlers were, first of all, functional. They were loose fitting and constructed of soft materials for ease of movement. This creation for the Kornitz Pure Oil team of Milwaukee, the WIBC champs in 1939 and 1947, demonstrates this, and features a horse-and-rider print, slit sleeves, button front, and is made of silk and cotton with immaculate hand embroidery.

Many manufacturers produced their shirts under specialty labels, some of the most popular being Hilton, Crown Prince, Nat Nast, King Louie, Hale-Niu, and Weber. Others were bought off the rack, or custom cut, and then hand decorated.

After the gilded age of the '50s and '60s, shirts fashioned from cheaper fabrics such as polyester, poplin, and sheeting, with screen-print artwork and a golf-shirt cut, replaced these clever and artful creations.

Reports of The King's appearance at the bowling alley in Baton Rouge last night were grossly exaggerated.

A rayon Swingster shirt with bold, embroidered graphics.

Nat Nast, one of the leading bowling shirt labels, consistently produced high-quality workmanship, like this nutty example from El Cajon, California.

The LA Toros, of the failed National Bowling League, chose Nadine of California to create their Mexican-inspired, gray gabardine shirts. Hall of Fame star Steve Nagy, owner of this shirt, was the Bowler of the Year, 1952.

Pro champion Gene Gagliardi wore this very classy, functional, Nat Nast creation.

Hilton made this classy, vented, 1950s cotton model. (Collection of the author.)

High-quality satin plus great design equals top-of-the-line bowling wear. (Courtesy Off Broadway, Finders Keepers Antiques, and Bowling Hall of Fame and Museum.)

Above: Many shirts were designed for snap-on patches, like this graphic cow design.

Right: Colorful award patches decorate this wool "letter sweater," which is also featured on our cover.

The great
Pete Weber, of
St. Louis, bowled 300
in his first sanctioned
game at age
fifteen.

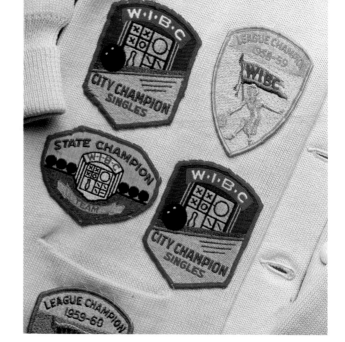

P A P A ' S   G O T   A   B R A N D   N E W   B A G

Bowling balls are heavy and unwieldy and can do serious damage if you let them get away from you! So, bowlers have come up with numerous contraptions over the years designed to lug the things back and forth to the alleys.

Wooden cratelike carrying boxes were popular in the late 1800s and early 1900s and are extreme rarities today. Certain other materials, such as canvas, were used for a time, but leather was the medium of choice through the 1940s, then vinyl in the '50s and '60s. Today you see mostly very practical, though boring and nondescript, nylon carriers.

Some bags were very ornate with artwork, often reminiscent of shirt-back designs, either printed or elaborately hand-tooled into the surface. After the introduction of special shoes, bags were normally designed larger to carry them and all the other essentials.

The better bowling bags were as well-designed and constructed as fine luggage, built to last a lifetime. They were prized possessions that came out of the closet and went down to the alley each week—a visual notice that the carrier was a force to be contended with!

63

A survivor of many trips to the lanes, this black leather bag dates from the 1940s.

Below: Functional, hard leather bags of this type were common during the early 1900s. This one from the '30s features a no-frills design and industrial-strength hardware. It's shown with a vintage Brunswick Mineralite ball and contemporary shoes.

Opposite, top right: A bowling kitsch collector's dream, this faux leopard skin bag with "bone" handle is a recent Flintstones thirtieth-anniversary promo item from Hanna-Barbera.

Opposite, top left: Probably from the 1950s, this exquisite hand-tooled leather bag of unknown origin is a real beauty, sporting a scene with deer on the side not shown.

Opposite, bottom: A collection of leather and vinyl bowling bags dated from the 1940s through the 1970s. Shown with an AMF Strikeline ball and Amflite pin.
(Collection of Off Broadway and the author.)

IF THE SHOE FITS . . .

Specially designed bowling shoes appeared in the 1920s and quickly became a necessity for the nattily dressed kegler. For many casual bowlers, shoes, like the balls, were simply rented at the bowling center, as they are today.

Avid bowlers, however, are quite serious about their footwear, often using a favorite, well-fitting pair for decades. The sliding foot—the left for right-handers—has a hard, slippery sole and a rubber heel that acts as a brake when it comes down. The other sole is conventional, without a rubber heel.

Like vintage baseball cleats, ballet slippers, or cowboy boots, these very personal, well-worn items seem somehow to preserve the character of their owners better than anything else associated with the sport.

Two-tone low-tops were just the ticket in the '40s and '50s.

Bought in 1942 for $3.50, these shoes were worn by their owner for 31 years.

Brunswick produced this fashion look in the '60s and '70s.

Tasteful gold lamé—just right for bowling in Las Vegas.

Three-time WIBC Champion and Hall of Famer Anita Cantaline bronzed her favorite pair.

These sturdy bowling sandals are from Kool Shuz, 1950s.

TINY BILLBOARDS

Bowling establishments have made liberal use of the lowly matchbook in their promotions over the years. Most often they were produced in very large quantities and distributed freely to patrons. The design of these tiny billboards, typically generated by nameless printshop production artists, ranged from the pedestrian use of one-color clip-art adaptations, to large and elaborate four-color-process productions.

Matchbooks often promoted the health benefits of bowling (never mind the implied use of tobacco) and the family-style fun of the sport, as well as advertised the features of the lanes. Air conditioning, obviously, was a major consideration for these all-season sport complexes, as was the availability of food and cocktails and luxurious surroundings. Of course, "robotic" pinsetting was a huge selling point in the era when rapid and efficient automation was replacing the outdated, manual pinboys.

Many matchbooks featured stylish depictions of the building exteriors, while others pictured the proprietors or famous customers. Whatever the particular message might be, these cost-effective, folding broadsides are examples of some of the most graphically exciting bowling advertisements.

COLLECTIBLE KITSCH

We have Mexican artesanos to thank for this silver and brass cigarette/music box from the 1950s. Gracias!

As a collector of ashtrays myself, I believe I have the authority to declare these two from the '40s and '50s—tacky!

70

The top half of this wonderful, well-made,
steel Deco cocktail server lifts off to
reveal a pump decanter and six shotglasses —
a bowling kitsch masterpiece.
(Collection of the author.)

FLASH!
BOWLING GAME

未瓶游戏

BATTERY POWERED **BOWLING SAVING BANK**

TEN PINS

Toy manufacturers have come up with innumerable variations on the bowling theme over the years, many of which are hilarious kitsch items, and others that are actually well-designed and challenging. These adorable toys are the forerunners of the bowling-related pinball and computer games of today. This collection of boxed games includes two sets from ca. 1920s, a bank from the 1970s, and a Japanese game, date unknown.

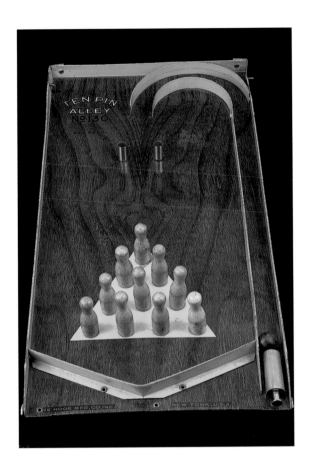

Above: Pinball wizards would love the approximately one-foot-long Tenpin Alley game from Hoge Manufacturing in New York ca. 1930s.

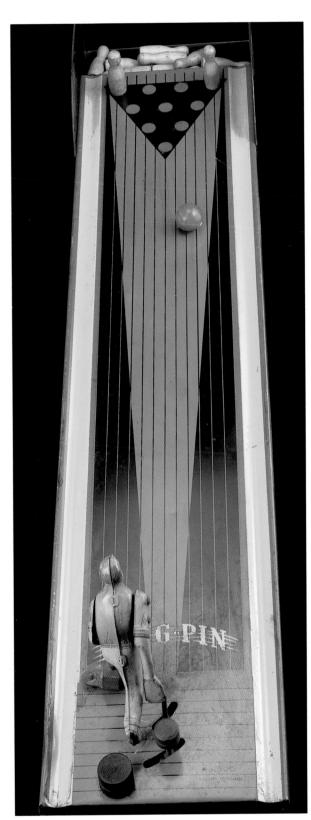

Right: With King Pin, from the '40s, Mr. Bowler has a two-foot lane on which to make those impossible spares.

Low-brow
gutter humor
becomes collectible
kitsch.

74

The Bowling
Hall of Fame and
Museum in St. Louis
boasts this
permanent display
of toys.

This collection of writing instruments and key chains includes advertising pens from the ABC, AMF, Brunswick, and others. Note the three-piece set awarded by Sheaffer's to Don Carter and the Brunswick scoring pen and pencil from days long gone.

The record for the most 300 games in one day is held by Troy Ockerman of Owassa, Michigan — four in one day!

The highest beginner's first-game league score ever bowled was a 253 by Bud Terrell of Bloomfield, Iowa, in 1974.

The sport of bowling, like most organized sports, very much likes to commemorate special events, to present awards for victory and exceptional achievement.

Trophies, plaques, pins, patches, badges, watches and jewelry, belt buckles, clocks... you name it... have always been presented to participants and winners of both pro and amateur events.

Host cities, as well as the ABC, WIBC, BPAA and other professional groups, often manufactured ornate souvenirs, awards and badges, which are today highly sought collector's items. The quality of the design, the materials and workmanship in many of these items, especially in the early years, was exceptional.

Silver, bronze, pewter, even gold and the occasional diamond were not unusual. Many trophies and awards were well-designed, often one-of-a-kind objects that exhibited sculptural integrity, while maintaining, in many instances, a slight whimsical quality typical of visuals associated with the sport. Other items, such as pins, badges and jewelry were worn with pride by men and women keglers alike. They were modest keepsakes and dignified symbols of a job well done.

A miniature replica of the perpetual ABC Masters Invitational Trophy at the National Bowling Hall of Fame.

Trophy Clock
awarded to Don
Carter in 1956.

A silver and
copper Cup
from 1910.

During the Glory Days of the fifties many awards and trophies, like these two, were quite stylish with elements of pewter, brass and wood.

PENN REC CLASSIC
1957-CHAMPION
JUNIE McMAHON
237-195-204-300-232
1168
TOURNEY RECORD

HIGH IND. AVE.
-1956-
JOE SINKE
-200-

During the Glory Days of the fifties many awards and trophies, like this group, were quite stylish with elements of pewter, brass and wood.

WIBC Hall of Fame bowler Betty Kuhl received this handsome trophy utilizing bakelite in its design for a 300 game in 1950.

This sophisticated
piece from the 1930s
utilized silver plate
and wood.

B O W L I N G   P I N S

A collection of host-city souvenir pins celebrate the special attributes of each locale.

The Beat Goes On

BY THE LATE SIXTIES, THE MAJOR downturn in the bowling industry, brought on by excess capacity and a radically changing social milieu, had pretty much bottomed out. Throughout the decade, thousands of bowling centers perished as interest on all levels waned.

Practically all the major pro teams disbanded, and the sport's two biggest competitive events were halted: the World Invitational in 1965 and the BPAA All-Star in 1970. Bowling's grand attempt to organize and televise a national team structure, the National Bowling League (NBL), was a miserable flop in 1961 – 62.

The oldest men's league bowler, through 1993, was John Venturello of Sunrise, Florida, a vigorous 105 that year.

The sad truth is, once the networks brought sophistication to their live-action coverage, bowling simply could not compete on a national level with the big-bucks, spectator sports—football, baseball, and basketball. So, the grim reality of the situation forced a massive shakeout in the industry—but it was by no means a death knell for the sport.

Bowling, like many recreational pursuits of the mid-twentieth-century techno-culture, had to find its niche to survive. That format turned out to be the Professional Bowlers Association (PBA), begun single-handedly in 1958 by a determined lawyer/sportscaster, Eddie Elias of Akron, Ohio. With lucrative ABC-TV contracts, the PBA Tour was able to provide income for the great pro bowlers like Dick Weber, Don Carter, Carmen Salvino, Steve Nagy, and Lou Campi—and at the same time keep the sport before the public.

86

The bowling industry learned to wholeheartedly embrace its constituency, to unashamedly declare itself the sport of the people—the middle-class answer to golf.

TV Guide reported in 1969 that "according to the ratings, almost every time it goes head-to-head against the prestigious game of golf, bowling knocks it into the creek. . . . The reason is simple. Golf may enjoy stature among the upper crust, but bowling has four times as many participants."

Showboat Lanes in Las Vegas, Nevada, as of press time, is the nation's largest bowling center, with 106 lanes.

Lasting Trends

Several trends became apparent throughout the sixties and seventies, and continued into the eighties and nineties. Mixed doubles—two men and two women—became the dominant league format, representing about 70 percent of sanctioned leagues by 1980. The trip to the bowling center increasingly became a casual date night more than a serious sporting event.

As a matter of fact, all league play went on a steady decline. Classic leagues all but disappeared; emphasis was definitely shifted to the casual

BOWLERS JOURNAL INTERNATIONAL

87

BOWLERS JOURNAL INTERNATIONAL

Above: Bold graphics and color enliven the newly redecorated Leisure Time center located within New York City's Port Authority Terminal.

Left: Airport Plaza Bowl, in Bethalto, Illinois, glistens with the featured use of chrome, glass bricks, and mirrors.

bowler and the social aspects of the game. Bowlers on an average became more sub-urban and older, with the general graying of the population.

Bowling made its debut as a medal sport event recognized by the Olympic Committee at the Pan American games in 1911.

Here's the good news—we are still talking about huge numbers! About 79 million people went bowling in the U.S. in 1993. Bowling, by far, is still the most popular participatory sport in the country. Though league interest has waned in recent years, the industry is surprisingly healthy in the mid-1990s. Exciting new pro stars, expansive cable and network coverage, and revived interest in international competition all add up to a good prognosis for the future.

Increasing youth involvement is another excellent indication. Formed in 1982 to promote youth league play, the Young American Bowling Alliance (YABA), with around 600,000 members, is the second-largest dues-paying youth sports organization in the world, behind only youth soccer.

Bowling continues to gain momentum as an international competitive sport as well. More than eighty-five countries enjoy American tenpins, and there is little doubt that it will soon be recognized as a sanctioned Olympic sport.

Responding in the 1990s to the demands of a visually sophisticated and more upscale customer base, bowling center architecture is suddenly very hot—again. The low-ceilinged, dark "alley" architecture of the sixties and seventies is out; light, airy, and very colorful postmodern structures are in.

New designs emphasize the "total entertainment" nature of the centers. Lighting is extremely important, with lots of neon and glass bricks especially incorporated into grand entranceways. Round columns are common, as are food courts with trendy seating, track lighting, and plenty of plants.

Of course, the newest centers are high tech, featuring the latest advancements in equipment, scoring, computer game analysis, and TV screens. Some centers incorporate Putt-Putt Golf, video-game arcades, and other diversions like the old standby, pool.

The year 1995 marked the hundredth anniversary of the American Bowling Congress, and an eighteen-month birthday party was planned. As ABC's Bowling Magazine reported, ". . . with cherished memories of . . . the bowlers of a century past fresh on our minds, we pay a lasting tribute to all those who laid the foundation for our great sport."

Hollywood Bowl in Stockton-on-Tees, England, radiates a fanciful energy inside and out with neon colors, sweeping, uncluttered lines, and classy furnishings.

BOWLERS JOURNAL INTERNATIONAL

89

BOWLERS JOURNAL INTERNATIONAL

Denmark's Super Bowling Aarhus features a dramatic entrance of white steel and glass.

A dazzling new National Bowling Stadium was erected in Reno, Nevada, to house the year's numerous anniversary events. The five-tiered structure is truly a marvel. Covering a full city block, it features eighty lanes in a row, seating for 1,200 spectators, and an Omnimax Theater dome. The world's largest rear-projection TV screen/scoreboard spans the 440-foot-long play area.

In this era of massive media hype and sports overkill, bowling continues to roll along in its friendly, unassuming fashion, a mature sport of unchallenged integrity. Bowling, with its accessibility to all and wholesome heroes, with its fun-loving image and joyful sense of humor, is an indelible part of our collective culture and a reminder of what sports is supposed to be all about.

90

COURTESY AND © LONNIE PECK, RENO NEWS BUREAU

Inside National Bowling Stadium in Reno, Nevada.

Outside the National
Bowling Stadium.

Photographs by
Michael Neese

Acknowledgments

A heartfelt thank you to my editor, Madge Baird, at Gibbs Smith, Publisher, who took a big chance on this first-time author; to Mike and Shelle Neese, my great friends and collaborators on this project, and to Douglas Egbert, their assistant at Studio Seven; to John Dalzell, curator extraordinaire at the National Bowling Hall of Fame and Museum in beautiful St. Louis, Missouri; and to my wife, Judi, for her support during my "bowling ball head" frenzies.

Thanks also to Off Broadway and Finders Keepers Antiques in Albuquerque for their gracious loan of objects; to Judy Sybertz and the other folks at Gary Skidmore's Holiday Bowl in Albuquerque; to Jim Dressel, Lydia Rypcinski and Karl Lueders at *Bowler's Journal*; to Pauline Testerman at the Truman Library; to Adrian Sakowicz and Eugene Fisher at Brunswick; to Rosie Crews with BPAA; to Chris Bame at the PBA; to Jennifer Kress at YABA; to Tom Parker at AMF; to Nat Andriani with Wide World Photos; to Lonnie Peck, Reno News Bureau.

The bowling statistics throughout the book were gleaned from *The Bowler's Almanac*, ©1994 American Bowling Congress and Women's International Bowling Congress. At the time of this writing, the most recent statistical figures available were for 1993.

For photographs, I especially want to thank Executive Director Gerald Baltz and Curator of Collections John Dalzell at the Bowling Hall of Fame and Museum in St. Louis. Without John's expert help and guidance at every step along the way, this book simply could not have been possible. He generously allowed unlimited access to the extensive collections of the museum and personally worked side by side with me for days to bring these rarely seen vintage photos and objects to the public (and he's not a bad photo assistant). Unless otherwise noted, all archival photography is courtesy of the Bowling Hall of Fame and Museum, and all original photography is by the author, except where noted otherwise.

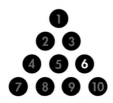

Selected Bibliography

Bush, Donald J. The Streamlined Decade. New York: George Braziller, Inc., 1975.

Hess, Alan. Googie, Fifties Coffee Shop Architecture. San Francisco: Chronicle Books.

Hickok, Ralph. Encyclopedia of North American Sports History. New York and Oxford: Facts on File, 1992.

Luby, Mort, Jr. The History of Bowling. Chicago: Luby Publishing, 1983.

Nash, Bruce, and Allan Zullo. Gutter Humor. Kansas City: Andrews and McMeel, 1994.

Nelson, Ray. A History of the ABC. Greendale, WI: American Bowling Congress, 1984.

Ritter, Lawrence. The Glory of Their Times. New York: William Morrow and Company, 1984.

Salvino, Carmen, with Frederick C. Klein. Fast Lanes. Chicago: Bonus Books, 1988.

Schunk, Carol. Bowling. Philadelphia: W. B. Saunders Company, 1976.

Talor, Dawson. How To Talk Bowling. New York: Dembner Books, 1987.

Weiskopf, Herman. The Perfect Game. Englewood Cliffs, NJ: Prentice-Hall, Inc., 1978.